TEN LANDSCAPES

ROCKPORT

TEN LANDSCAPES

MICHAEL BALSTON

EDITED BY JAMES GRAYSON TRULOVE

ROCKPORT PUBLISHERS

First published in the United States of America by:

Rockport Publishers, Inc.
33 Commercial Street
Gloucester, Massachusetts 01930-5089
Telephone: (978) 282-9590
Facsimile: (978) 283-2742
www.rockpub.com

ISBN: 1-56496-785-9

10 9 8 7 6 5 4 3 2 1
Cover Image: Jerry Harpur
Printed in China.

James Grayson Trulove is a magazine and book pub-
lisher and editor in the fields of landscape architec-
ture, art, graphic design, and architecture. He has pub-
lished, written, and edited over 30 books including,
most recently, *New Design: Berlin, New Design:
Amsterdam, Designing the New Museum, Dancing in the
Landscape: The Sculpture of Athena Tacha,* and *The New
American Swimming Pool.* Trulove is a recipient of the
Loeb Fellowship from Harvard University's Graduate
School of Design. He resides in Washington, D.C.

FOREWORD

by Christopher Lloyd

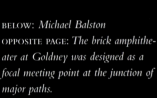

Michael Balston loves nothing better than to work on a large scale; he gets excited by a job, is laudably attentive to his clients' tastes and requirements, makes lasting friendships with them and he likes to be able to follow and continuingly develop a project throughout the years. His flair and creativity have long impressed me and I never fail to be stimulated when we meet, for we have known each other for more than twenty years.

Ten Gardens gives us varied samples of a range of mainly private gardens, large and small, urban and country, that he has created or developed. No project is daunting to him, be it private or public, and he is quite evidently able to inspire his clients. Always, he likes to use the best materials. If a tennis court or a swimming pool is needed, it is no obstructive eyesore to him. He knows how to integrate it harmoniously.

He is acutely conscious of the relationship of building to garden and vice versa, and house plans have not infrequently been modified at his suggestions to tie in with the garden. He is particularly sensitive towards the historic continuity of a site, as exemplified in his work at Goldney Hall in Bristol, or Little Malvern Court in Worcestershire. He sees his work as another layer in an evolving story. Best of all, perhaps, is when he can assess and make a start on the garden before major additions to the house have been

He is great on the manipulation of slopes, the making of retaining walls and ha-ha's, but perhaps even greater is his love of introducing a lake into the landscape. He is skilled in the manipulation of all such projects. And yet, even in a tiny and superficially unpromising town garden, largely at basement level, he has made something satisfying and unfussed.

And what about plants, the plantsmen among us must ask? His detailed knowledge of plants, he would be the first to admit, is not that of a nurseryman, but he knows the bold and the beautiful and his plant knowledge is increasing all the time. He does not, like so many land-scape designers, find plants a nuisance, because they are living and unpredictable. He loves good planting and is a most rewarding person to take into my own garden. And his own is large. In it he is always experimenting; it is only time that limits his input there.

Michael's Daily Telegraph-sponsored gar-den for the 1999 Chelsea Flower Show, deservedly won the highest award for the garden of that year (not that the judges necessarily knew any more about the subject than I do!). Using the most modern (and hideously expen-sive) yet brilliantly, effective materials available, the steel structure looked deceptively simple and the light canvas canopies made it seem almost airborne. The slanting design made it the more spacious and the water canal was both lively and restful. All credit to the Royal Horticultural Society for transferring this garden to add to their examples of small gardens at Wisley, where it sits a lot more comfortably on a slope and can be sensibly planted to take account of the seasons.

I am no garden designer myself and I have almost certainly not done sufficient justice to Michael's genius, but it is important that landscape work of this kind should be seen, assessed and criticized by the public at large, who are its ultimate users. I have no hesitation about hailing Michael Balston's work as some of the most forward-looking to be seen and revelled in today. A garden, he believes, "should not only be able to cope with change, but should actually welcome it. Gardening is a temporal art as well as a spatial one. Gardeners should be encouraged to experiment with plants. My role as a designer is to provide an inspiring structure within which these plants are used." Hear, hear to all that, but few designers would express themselves with such modesty.

It is the open-minded, experimental mentality that we most need, and less of harking back.

Christopher Lloyd has written more than a dozen books on gardening and plants. His latest book is *Christopher Lloyd's Garden Flowers*, an encyclopedia of perennials, bulbs, grasses, and ferns. He is a regular contributor to *Country Life* magazine as well as many other publications.

ABOVE: *Although the ha-ha is designed for an outward view, with expert craftsmanship it can be an important design feature when viewed inward as seen here at Heather's Farm.*

OPPOSITE PAGE, TOP LEFT: *The circular pool picks up the Hall's geometry of towers and windows.*
OPPOSITE PAGE, LEFT: *In the student accommodations at Goldney Hall, ease of maintenance is a key consideration.*

MANOR FARM HOUSE

The garden at my home in Wiltshire is the one that has taught me the most about the craft of gardening. Since 1983 I have learned how to grow my own plants in a relatively large garden over a long period of time where I have sole control. I now understand so much more about the business of garden management, how to encourage and control growth, how to direct labor, about the use of chemicals and machinery. There is only a certain amount that you can learn from courses, text books or other people's gardens. In your own you live with your mistakes or you root them out and start again. It has also taught me more about exploiting location and the environmental aspects of the Genius of the Place. The shelter of walls and southerly elevations of the building may appear obvious, but there are surprising subtleties that can seldom be discovered by a visiting designer. Some things are only apparent after constant observation.

When I started on our family garden, I was more architect than gardener. More concerned with space and geometry, I wanted to control the planting so that it rigidly reinforced the organizing principles of the garden. Now I am more relaxed about the planting and I realize that the organizing thrust of the design, together with its interlocking spaces, is so strong that almost anything can happen in the planting. This is just as well as I am now keenly interested in chance—the things in gardens that happen by themselves. Seed being blown about into unplanned places can produce some felicitous harmonies or indeed challenging contrasts. The odd bit of disease can produce a host of intriguing opportunities. I conclude that Fate should be a gardener's friend. And the interplay between chance and design is pretty exciting.

ABOVE: *Sculpture is an important part of the garden. This stone apple is located under an apple tree in the orchard.*

The garden's layout is determined by an axis through front and back doors of the house up into the walled garden and field beyond. At the southerly end, close to where my office is now located, we have put a focal urn of my own design, on a pedestal—all pretty traditional, but which suits the essentially eighteenth century farm house. At the northerly end of the axis is a conical mount clad in box and with a spiral path winding round. This is a rather more modern response though still an idea that has been around for the last 5,000 years, at least in Wiltshire although this was only created in 1990, I knew in 1983 that a mount would be an essential part of the composition. Off the central axis are arranged smaller spaces that all have their own special character, exhibiting different colors and textures.

The garden divides into five major themes. The front is relatively formal with pleached hornbeams round a rectangular croquet lawn and a box and peony parterre in the front of the house. While the box has grown steadily, the infilling has gone through many evolutions on account of the particularly difficult growing environment half under the canopy of an enormous *Quercus ilex*.

To the rear is the walled garden. On our arrival in 1983 there were a few old apple trees and a ramshackle shed in this space. We removed the shed and created a stone paved courtyard at the rear of the house that makes a wonderfully protected outdoor dining room on sunny days. This leads up steps to an oval lawn followed by a rectangular lawn and then to the still unfinished shell house that makes a gateway from the walled garden into the kitchen garden. The walled garden is planted with small trees, shrubs, including roses and some herbaceous material and underplanted with spring bulbs. It is far from complete, continuing to evolve and my long-term plan has water and stone in place of the rectangular lawn in front of the shell house.

The third area is the kitchen garden, originally carved out of the southern end of the field. This is not large but seems to supply an almost inexhaustible quantity of vegetables, far more than our actual requirements. It is enclosed by the remains of the mud wall and the thorn hedge and is now twice its original size thanks to a splendid gale in 1990 that blew over a poplar inconsiderately growing in the western half of the garden.

Beyond is the fourth section, the field that contains the mount and a pond. As I write it is foaming with cow parsley, punctuated liberally with blue *Camassia*. Growing up through are vestigial hay meadow grasses, dogstail, cocksfoot, timothy, bents and so on. I let the grass grow on until late July or early August when it gets cut. There are then a couple more cuts, weather permitting, in the autumn before the emergence of the *Colchicums* and *Crocus speciosus*. During spring and summer, paths are cut through the growing grass, which is liberally studded with spring bulbs and summer flowers. The herb layer swirls through a collection of trees that I planted in the 1980s that are now up to 30 feet high in some cases. This is perhaps my favorite part of the garden, where almost all is left to chance.

ABOVE: *These pyramids are for climbing roses and clematis. They provide a focal contrast to the foliage and gave instant height to the garden when it was new.*

The fifth section is occupied by a tennis court and herbaceous border located on ground acquired in 1996. I was determined to make a court that could form a focal space in the garden instead of being tucked away behind a hedge. So we levelled the area, built the court and surrounded it with an oak cloister that is now beginning to make a stout frame for climbing plants. Instead of the more usual chain-link fence, we used a fine nylon net that is almost invisible against the stout oak columns supporting it. Along one side is a mixed border, supported by background shrubs such as *Viburnum, Buddleia, Sambucus, Photinia* and punctuated in the foreground by large clumps of *Cortaderia, Miscanthus* and other grasses. On the opposite side is an orchard on an enclosing bank.

I am grievously short of time in the garden at the moment, being too much occupied with other people's gardens, but sooner or later I will spend more there, and experiment and learn more about plants. Perhaps, too, I will overlay the basic design with new ideas in modern materials, demonstrating the multi-layered nature of an evolving garden. Gardening is a temporal art as well as a spatial one, and I look forward to continuing change.

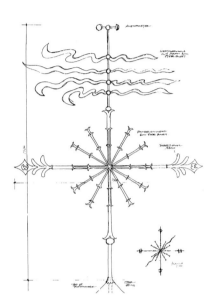

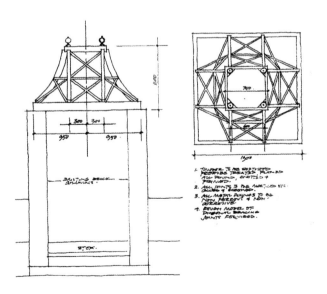

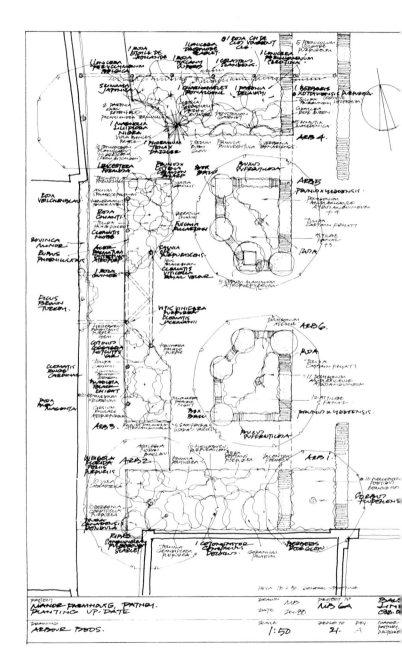

ABOVE: *The shell house and kitchen garden as seen over cow parsley from the mount.*

LEFT: *The central axis through the shell house and kitchen garden looking up towards the field. The succession of spaces leads the eye through to the field.*

OPPOSITE PAGE, CLOCKWISE FROM TOP LEFT: *Sketch for weather vane; partial garden plan; sketch for rose arbor.*

RIGHT: *The box-clad mount with a yew on top. The shape of the yew is still to be worked out—unless it stays as an erupting volcano.*

LEFT: *A portion of the herbaceous bor-der with* Achillea grandiflora, *a magnificent but under-used border plant.*

ABOVE: *A paving detail from the shell house created by the gardener Rod Gale.*

LEFT: *The front of the house is swathed with wisteria and roses and overlooks a formal layout of box and santolina.*

OPPOSITE PAGE: *A view through to the oval lawn from the vine clad arbor with* Helleborus x sternii *and* Daphne pontica *in the gap.*

ABOVE: *A sitting area in the walled garden in spring with Tulip Magier and Angelique performing wonderfully.*

RIGHT: *A temporary wild flower area on a recently disturbed bank near the tennis court.*

OPPOSITE PAGE: *The new border along the edge of the tennis court. The plinths are left over from a flower show and flank a sitting area.*

LITTLE MALVERN COURT

My earliest long-term relationship with a site began at Little Malvern Court, a large house in the Malvern hills with long views over the Severn Valley towards the Cotswolds. I continued this job from my former partnership with fellow garden designer Arabella Lennox-Boyd. By 1983 Arabella and I had got the bones of the job planned, so from then on I was largely concerned with detailed planning, construction and planting, planning the next phases and then management.

It was really to Arabella Lennox-Boyd that I owed my introduction to gardens. As a landscape architect, I had originally worked on large-scale civic projects with my mentors Hugh Morris and Maurice Lee of Robert Matthew Johnson-Marshall and Partners, a large firm of architects, engineers and planners. Arabella and I joined forces in 1978 and we worked together until 1983 when I moved to Wiltshire. Her practice provided a novel opportunity for me to work for private clients and to become more horticultural. This partly precipitated my departure to the country to get more hands-on experience in my own garden. She had a good eye and a sure touch as well as being an inspiring companion and I learned much during my time with her.

ABOVE: *Circular steps provide access through the retaining wall and allow views from the library down to the lake.*
OPPOSITE PAGE, FAR RIGHT: *Design for plant training wires.*
OPPOSITE PAGE, RIGHT: *Garden plan.*

The house is medieval in foundation and of some literary significance since here is where William Langland wrote his allegorical poem *Piers Plowman* in about 1370. It was much altered since its monastic days, particularly by Joseph Hanson, of horse-drawn cab fame, for in the nineteenth century, he completely remodeled the northern end. In 1983, there was a particularly barren sweep of lawn around the building and a magnificent lime tree on the south-east corner. There was a substantial pond, probably a monastic fish pond in origin, though recently altered. I was intrigued to unravel the history, and archival research turned up evidence of a chain of ponds. As the existing pond sat uncomfortably on the hillside, we restored the ponds to their original levels with weirs between them with an elm bridge across. At the changes in level we planted banks of shrubs and herbaceous plants with aquatics and marginals nearby in the water.

With level platforms created by a major new retaining wall, a traditional compartmented layout evolved around the house enclosed by yew hedges, pear espaliers and pleached limes. To the north was a garden of old-fashioned roses supplemented with Chinese junipers, hydrangeas and lots of bulbs for the spring. On a key junction of the paths a timber arbor made a focus that looks spectacular festooned in white climbing roses. In time, I extended the gardens south around the old Priory church and north to the spring, where the main water supply to the lake enters. There a bowl was scooped out of the side of the hill and large rocks brought in to create a tumble of stone with the water running through into the top pond.

This was a germinal work for me and I have been involved there now for nearly twenty years. I have learned much through the kindness of my clients and collaborators in the development of this garden.

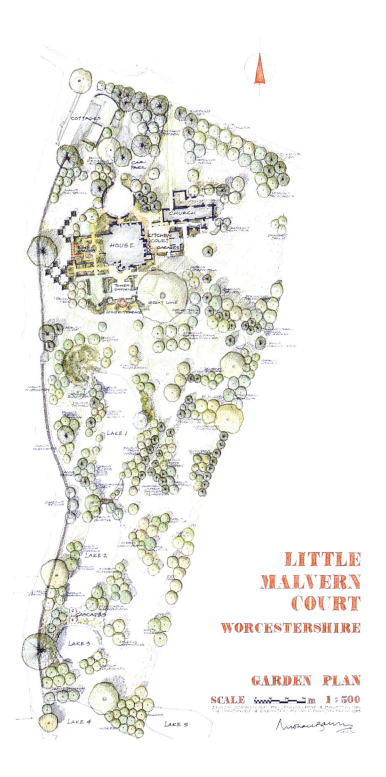

COTTAGES

CAR PARK

CHURCH

KITCHEN COURT

HOUSE

GARAGES

TOWER GARDEN

GREAT LIME

LOWER TERRACE

LAKE 1

LAKE 2

CASCADES

LAKE 3

LAKE 4

LAKE 5

LITTLE MALVERN COURT
WORCESTERSHIRE

GARDEN PLAN

SCALE ⊢━━━━┤m 1 : 500

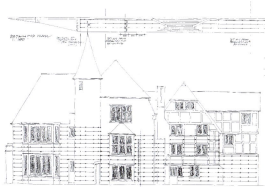

HOUSE - SOUTH ELEVATION (1 : 100)

CLOCKWISE FROM TOP LEFT: *The lower border below the retaining wall that separates the upper garden from the lawns to the south; the cascade flows southward over timber sleepers with clay between, towards the second and third pond; brick garden with box and yew hedges that give definition in the winter when bulbs and annuals are not evident.*

OPPOSITE PAGE: *Umbrellas of* Prunus 'Ukon' *with trimmed yew hedges beyond.*

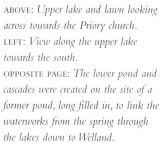

ABOVE: *Upper lake and lawn looking across towards the Priory church.*

LEFT: *View along the upper lake towards the south.*

OPPOSITE PAGE: *The lower pond and cascades were created on the site of a former pond, long filled in, to link the waterworks from the spring through the lakes down to Welland.*

JANNAWAYS

One of my earliest jobs having established my own in practice 1983, was executed for Christopher and Sharon Sharples at their London house. They responded well to my ideas and seemed to like the way I went about things. So when they acquired Jannaways, not the most prepossessing of 1930's suntrap houses and deeply overshadowed by vast trees that blocked out both morning and afternoon sun, they kindly asked me to try and help them sort out the immediate problems as well as to plan for the future.

Close to a little tributary of the River Lambourn, the house sits on a chalk slope running down to the stream. With clay at the bottom, boggy areas of peat had formed, making much of the garden extremely wet and virtually unusable. I, therefore, proposed turning most of the garden into a lake—a proposal that my clients bravely acceded to. We could use the spoil from the lake to create a grass terrace for croquet and party marquees—the only flat area on the whole site, apart from the terraces outside the house.

The lake eventually comprised about a third of the garden. The flow of ground water was sufficient to keep it always full and it has become the focus of the garden. At the same time, we built a stone terrace following the line of the house, with two arms projecting out towards tile-roofed, open-sided pavilions overlooking the water. The arms embrace a lower terrace, also in stone, laced through with a brick pattern that picks up the geometry of the building. The idea was to extend the house outward, creating an open-sided outdoor court. This completely transformed the appearance of the original structure making something spacious and elegant out of an otherwise somewhat pedestrian elevation.

All this was part of a longer term development plan that determined spaces for a tennis court, a swimming pool and a kitchen garden, among other things. Although none of these became reality for some time, a strategy for the whole site meant that the work could be carried out in the future as part of a coherent design. Advance planting of trees and hedges ensured that the site structure matured even though the detailed planting came later.

The planting needed to suit the varied conditions ranging from the boggy lower ground to dry shallow chalk on the north side of the house. We planted many native trees that have prospered and ornamentals trees such as *Pterocarya* on the lake edge, *Betula jacquemontii*, *Liriodendron* and *Metasequoia*. Shrubs were chosen for season and color, though by this time I was beginning to appreciate more the value of texture, which was important in the large areas of marginal planting.

A good relationship developed with an enlightened client so that the work continues—even this year, (2000) we completed steps on the north side that were first mooted back in 1985. A successful garden should work well at a personal level as well as at an aesthetic and technical level.

FAR RIGHT: *A fountain at the end of the upper terrace.*
RIGHT: *Large seats are useful focal points. This one is in the middle of one side of the lower terrace.*
BELOW: *Plan for ornamental pool and seating area.*
OPPOSITE PAGE: *Garden plan.*

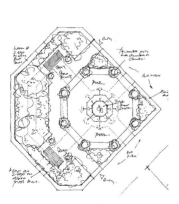

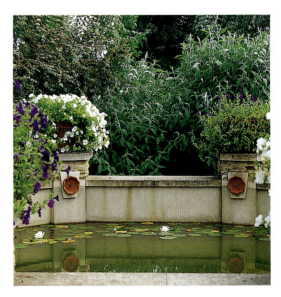

JANNAWAYS, BAGNOR, BERKSHIRE

DEVELOPMENT PLAN

SCALE 1:250

RIGHT: *The pavilions are built to match the details of the house and serve to extend the living space.*
BELOW: *Sketch for garden pavilions.*

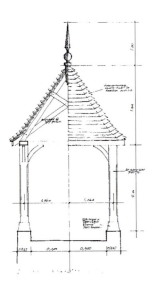

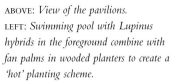

ABOVE: *View of the pavilions.*

LEFT: *Swimming pool with Lupinus hybrids in the foreground combine with fan palms in wooded planters to create a 'hot' planting scheme.*

ABOVE: *A long view over the lake giving the impression of a huge expanse of water.*

LEFT: *Water is as valuable for its reflections as for its movement. Here the lake becomes a mirror, reflecting autumn's colors.*

OPPOSITE PAGE: *House and pavilion as seen from the south boundary. The walk continues all the way around the lake.*

ROFFORD MANOR

Rofford Manor is perhaps the best known of my private gardens. My involvement came about in a curious way. Christopher Lloyd was being customarily irreverent about some of my more irrational (to him) thoughts about plants in one of his weekly articles for *Country Life*. Reading it, Hilary and Jeremy Mogford thought that I might be the person to help them. Thus began a long association that has spanned two private gardens and two hotel gardens.

Rofford Manor is a substantial traditional brick and tile house with outbuildings set on the flattish plain to the north west of the Chilterns. A kitchen garden and a herb garden were already in the making, and when I arrived on the scene borders were about to be started. The general proposals were entirely logical, and at this stage I merely tweaked what was already started and developed the planting plans. Even then I was attempting to introduce a slanting dynamic into otherwise symmetrical borders—a foretaste of Chelsea 1999 perhaps.

The next project was the swimming pool garden, where I tried to mitigate the baldness of the pool structure by planting close to the edges in raised stone planters. The billowing foliage breaks the hard line of the pool edge whilst modern cleaning gadgets are quite sufficient to pick up the odd leaf that drops in. Then came the green garden to the west side of the house in which the subtly different textures of yew and box and pleached limes in varying shades of green are a soothing contrast to the horticulture of the borders and rose garden.

The works have gone on over the years—improvements to the entrance court, the creation of a little gravel garden for the caretaker's cottage and a new greenhouse off the kitchen garden. They even rashly allowed me to interfere with the buildings, and I drew up a scheme for one of the barns as a banqueting hall. It was scarcely an economic use of an existing building but it made a wonderful place for a party. I advised, too, on the planting around the new lake in the low ground to the north west. With an extensive use of native species designed to encourage wildlife, we formed substantial new belts of trees that reshaped the spaces in a way that was more sympathetic to the natural lie of the land.

More recently we have extended the green garden to the west creating a large lawn retained by a long curving ha-ha to keep the cattle out. Overlooking and backing on to the rose garden is the new steep-roofed belvedere with views to the lake. This new work has drawn the entire garden together on the western side.

It has been a great satisfaction creating this garden with the Mogfords who work hard in the garden themselves. The creation has been truly a joint effort in which their contribution, in terms of ideas and sheer hard work, has complemented and reinforced mine. It is a model relationship that I believe has produced the best from all of us. If only it could happen more often.

RIGHT: *Pleached limes enclose the green garden.*
OPPOSITE PAGE, CLOCKWISE FROM LEFT: *Garden plan; aerial view of main entrance courtyard; main entrance and courtyard.*

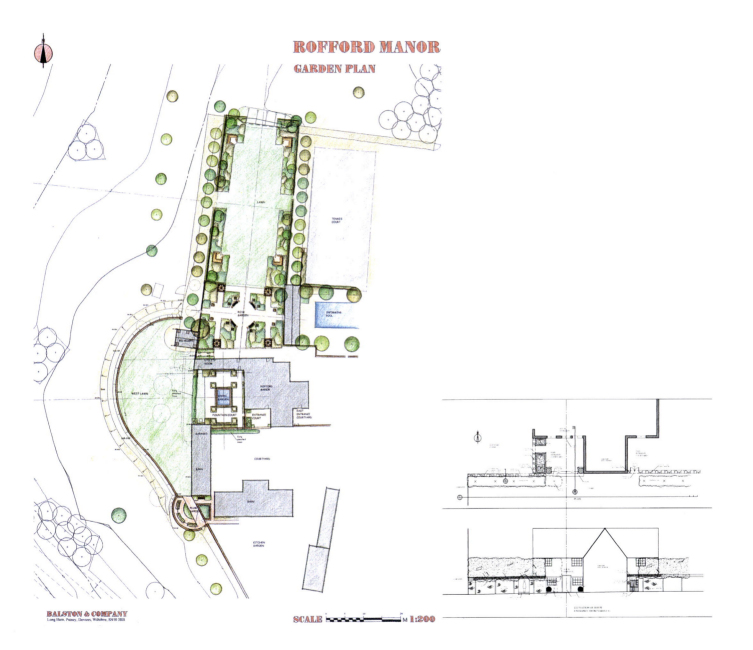

ROFFORD MANOR
GARDEN PLAN

BALSTON & COMPANY
Long Barn, Putney, Devizes, Wiltshire, SN10 3RB

SCALE M 1:200

ABOVE: *The path to the kitchen door through the green garden.*

LEFT: *Another area of clipped shrubs consisting of box and santolina in a rather more complex design on the east side of the house.*

OPPOSITE PAGE: *The restful green garden is dominated by clipped box and yew.*

RIGHT: *A view of the swimming pool through the pool house. The manipulation of light and shade is an essential part of the garden's design.*

BELOW: *Sketch of swimming pool and terrace.*

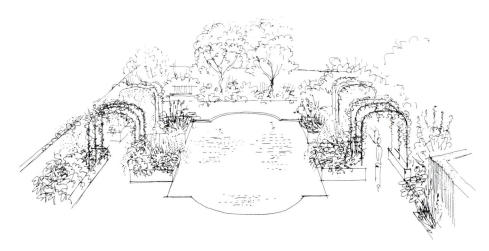

LEFT: *Clipped box in Versailles boxes are always useful in a garden at points of entry and exit.*

LEFT: *The rose garden that lies on the route to the swimming pool and the north-south axis of the garden. The obelisks are planted with clematis.*
OPPOSITE PAGE: *A casual way around the northeastern corner of the house where plants grow in the cracks in the paving.*

RIGHT: *The borders flanking the croquet lawn are designed to be at their peak as late in the season as possible.*
FOLLOWING PAGES: *The garden provides many places for rest and reflection.*

CUCKLINGTON HOUSE

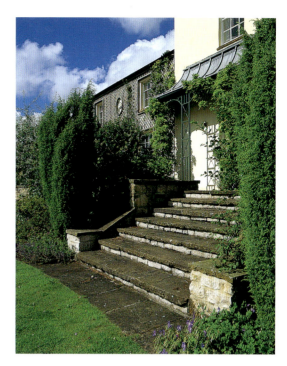

Overlooking the Blackmoor Vale in Somerset, Cucklington House is perched on the side of a steep escarpment. It has sumptuous views to the west over a patchwork of farmland that still has its hedges and its cows. But as so often in England, good south-westerly views let in the south-westerly gales and when the weather is boisterous, raindrops travel upwards on the windows.

My involvement in this job, as ever, was by a somewhat circuitous route and I was taken on because of my enthusiasm for flooding a field to make a lake. My megalomaniac tendencies would have flooded the whole Vale if I had had half a chance. My client had vision and appreciated my ideas. Design sessions were long and hotly argued, fuelled by copious wine and sumptuous food. The process ensured that he fully identified with a design that truly belonged to him and the house. Although tiring, it was a thoroughly rewarding process.

As domestic jobs go, it was pretty big but absolutely my kind of area, combining buildings and landscape. It required much attention both at the planning stage and in the detailed drawings and specifications. We started with a careful survey to work out precisely the best views and vantage points. The layout of the new buildings and gardens was firmly based on this visual analysis. As well as the garden and its structure, the brief included a large octagonal conservatory at the same level as the house and an indoor swimming pool half buried into the hillside below. There were miles of retaining wall to build, paving to put down and beds to prepare. A tennis court was installed near the swimming pool and the great ha-ha constructed that separated the garden from the fields below. Construction was against an incredibly tight program, and we got off to a bad start with the site being under snow for an unreasonable length of time. But we achieved enough of the building works to have a major round of shrub and herbaceous planting in the winter of 1993 to 1994 prior to our deadline—a felicitous deadline if ever there was one...

The great party of July 1994 made all the blood, sweat, and tears worthwhile. Through the client's French connections, the food and wine were choice. There was a French theme and two or three hundred guests, I forget now, wandered round the garden dressed as revolutionaries or French chambermaids in their little black numbers. Cartloads of oysters from Brittany opened the eating, followed by terrines and pates, lobsters and quails, red meat and white and beautifully cooked vegetables.

But that, of course, was not the end. The lake, the raison d'etre of my appointment, was created. Then came the kitchen garden to supply a growing family as well as the next party. What a project—it was wonderfully extravagant and it built as strong a friendship as it did a garden. I can only count myself lucky to have been involved in such an exciting scheme.

FAR RIGHT: *Sketch for conservatory pineapple finial.*
RIGHT: *Sketch of alterations to front door.*
OPPOSITE PAGE, CLOCKWISE FROM TOP: *Garden plan; watercolor showing view from kitchen garden toward school house; watercolor of water feature and pool.*

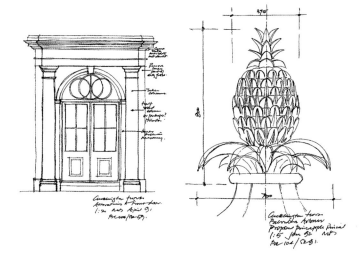

CUCKLINGTON HOUSE

GARDEN PLAN

SCALE 1:200

ABOVE: *An arbor in the kitchen garden beckons through the veranda terrace door.*

LEFT: *Textures were particularly exploited at Cucklington. This path is constructed in cobble stone.*

OPPOSITE PAGE: *A new door through an old wall leads to the veranda terrace.*

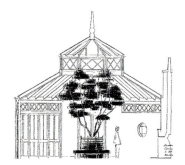

ABOVE: *Sketch of conservatory with central olive tree*

RIGHT: *The conservatory, constructed by Marston & Langinger, is a key element in the chain of structures from the house to the tennis court.*

ABOVE: *The circular window at the end of the conservatory passage becomes a focal point at the end of the croquet lawn.*

LEFT: *Particular attention was paid to the alignment and elevation of different features.*

LEFT: *Granite setts contrast with bricks where a path leads up to the greenhouse and garages.*

OPPOSITE PAGE: *The kitchen garden lies to the north of the house. An arbor marks a junction of the paths.*

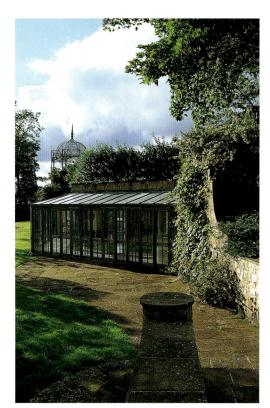

CLOCKWISE FROM TOP LEFT: *The glazed wall of the underground swimming pool with the belvedere prominent at the end; the view over the Blackmoor Vale from the belvedere is superb; at the northern end of the range of buildings is the old school house.*

OPPOSITE PAGE: *The house and some of its flanking buildings as seen from the lake below.*

HEATHER'S FARM

This job was the first that I carried out in conjunction with Joanna Wood, the interior designer, and Barrett Lloyd Davis, the architects. It was relatively ambitious in scope and based on a modest Sussex farmhouse and small-holding locked into large stretches of mature woodland. The landscape was agreeable and well-protected, but it had the disadvantage of being situated on the heaviest of mid-Sussex clays—positively a back-breaking site. However, the energetic Mr. and Mrs. Gregson were not in the least bit daunted and have turned it into a highly productive ground with ornamental and fruit trees racing away, a full kitchen garden and a big curved border that now looks almost mature. Again, I have been extraordinarily lucky with my clients, for they take advice and work hard to achieve the best possible result. Working in close collaboration with Joanna Wood and the architect we became a close knit team and the success of the overall scheme has owed as much to my clients input as it has to my own. A joint effort is so much more rewarding than lonely furrow ploughing.

Starting in late 1993 I found that works to the house were already under way, but that nobody had had much clue as to how the garden could or should be integrated. The drive and its flanking hedge followed an unfortunate route that divided the area around the house from the fields to the south. The key design gambit was to relocate the drive and break through the hedge into the field beyond. We then made a large circular lawn and enclosing it with a ha-ha, created the illusion of unimpeded space rolling away to the distant woods. This lawn formed the central feature around which the whole design revolved. It gave us the opportunity to create a long, curved, mixed border on the west side, `a la Anglesey Abbey, near Cambridge. I find this one of the most satisfactory ways of displaying a mixed bed as the relationship among groups of plants is constantly on the move as you walk around. From the mid-point of the border a route was made that led north through the newly created kitchen garden to a large greenhouse. West of this, against the boundary trees, we created a large, square sleeper-edged pond with a green oak pavilion on its axis. To the east of the circular lawn we terraced the rising ground into walks of cobnuts and walnuts that screened the farm buildings. Against the house we made a long stone terrace framing beds in which roses, *clematis*, jasmine, *eschscholzia* and *Solanum* luxuriate, along with myrtle, cistus and hebe.

The planting of the border was an interesting exercise. We backed it with a yew hedge planted with 60cm (2-feet) high plants, and now growing at 30cm (1-foot) a year. Behind we planted an orchard of apples, damsons and cherries, together with some ornamental trees. Structural plants in the border itself included *Amelanchier*, lilac, purple hazel, golden *Philadelphus*, *Forsythia suspensa* and many others. These were not chosen for their horticultural rarity–more for their good performance in the given conditions and their combination with the other plants. About sixty percent of the area was planted with summer herbaceous plants including such stars as *Crambe cordifolia*, irises and *Acanthus spinosus*, then *Macleaya cordata*, *Phlox paniculata* and *Eupatorium purpurea* that kept the flowering going well into the autumn. For the spring we inter planted with *Scilla*, *Chionodoxa*, *anenome*, and *crocus* with *Narcissus* behind in the orchard area. Then to hold it all together we spaced at regular intervals big clumps of *delphiniums* for the summer, *Cortaderia selloana* for the autumn and at a more closely spaced rhythm, *yucca* in the front. On the other side of the path, taking up the change in level to the circular lawn was a bank clad in box with *Crataegus oxycantha coccinea plena* planted at regular intervals. The border is conceived as a unit and highly structured but it has sufficient flexibility for the Gregsons to take it over and introduce their own plants in due course.

FAR RIGHT, RIGHT: *The curved border from the central arbor. The circular lawn lies to the left. The changing level of the border against the circular lawn is taken up by a box planted bank with standard thorns growing through.*
OPPOSITE PAGE, TOP: *Garden plan.*
OPPOSITE PAGE, BOTTOM: *Sketch of view across swimming pool.*

HEATHER'S FARM

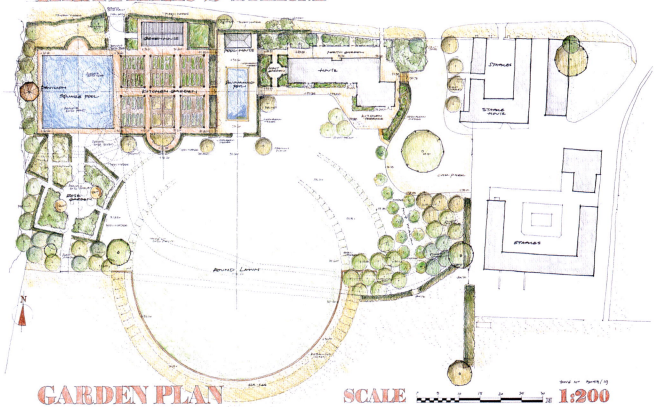

GARDEN PLAN

SCALE 1:200

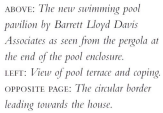

ABOVE: *The new swimming pool pavilion by Barrett Lloyd Davis Associates as seen from the pergola at the end of the pool enclosure.*
LEFT: *View of pool terrace and coping.*
OPPOSITE PAGE: *The circular border leading towards the house.*

ABOVE: *View through the kitchen garden to the pond arbor.*

RIGHT: *The pond arbor from the circular border.*

LEFT: *The pavilion overlooking the square pond.*

LOWER LYE

I have been lucky with some of the sites I have worked. Lower Lye is on the Wiltshire/Dorset border in the most sumptuous country. Lying in a ripple of ground on a southwesterly slope, the house has wonderful views towards Alfred's Tower above Stourhead to the west and over the Stour Valley. It is an inspiring site and my clients, Andrew and Belinda Scott, made the bold decision to rebuild part of the house and retain the site, rather than move elsewhere to accommodate their growing family more commodiously.

I was also fortunate in that I was appointed before they had re-planned the house, so that I could influence the siting and massing of its extension and of the outbuildings. The relationship of building to site is as much a landscape issue as an architectural one. How you approach a building, where the front door is, the space outside that welcomes the visitor, even the space inside the front door are all relevant to the journey through the landscape that terminates in the building. If these decisions are made irreversible before the landscape designer is consulted, then that journey can sometimes go badly wrong.

Nicky Johnson and Peter Cave were appointed architects and in a fruitful collaboration we planned a considerable complex of buildings and landscape that included the house, garages, a greenhouse and a swimming pool, as well as a croquet lawn and a grass tennis court and a rose garden. A building spine evolved along the contours with a garage court to the north and interlocking garden spaces opening out to the landscape. There was a strong sense of place and full advantage taken of the views.

Landscape works started in 1995, well in advance of the house, with the round lawn, sited at the end of the rose garden and looking out over a steep valley. Then we moved on to the drive. The old drive was direct and oblivious of the wonderful views that could be had from the higher ground. A re-routing of the drive could make the approach to the house really exciting. It was an expensive option but bravely agreed by Andrew and Belinda and inevitably it changed everyone's perception of the site. That complete, we immediately went into major earth-moving to get the site into shape before the works to the main building began. This afforded us the bonus of established grass areas before the house was re-occupied.

The planting, at least in the park, also had the advantage of an early start. We concentrated on natives like oak, lime and field maple, and supplemented them with more exotic species such as Black Walnut, Sweet gum, Tulip tree and Red Oak. The planting round the house, however, had to be delayed. Thus the rose garden, the big herbaceous border, the oval lawn and the walk down towards the round fountain had to wait until spring 1997. But growth has been good, and the garden is now looking reasonably mature with some of the more vigorous herbaceous plants ready for thinning. It will not be long before the garden will look as though it has been there forever, with its former layout a distant memory.

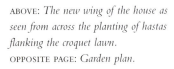

ABOVE: *The new wing of the house as seen from across the planting of hastas flanking the croquet lawn.*
OPPOSITE PAGE: *Garden plan.*

LOWER LYE PARK

BALSTON & COMPANY
Landscape Architects & Garden Designers

Long Barn, Potterne, Devizes, Wiltshire SN10 5RR

SCALE 1:500

N

LEFT: *The terrace adjacent to the old wing of the house.*
OPPOSITE PAGE: *The junction of the new and old wings as seen past the magnificent tulip tree that remained from the original garden.*

ABOVE: *A view through an existing beech hedge to a relocated urn.*
RIGHT: *A sundial at the junction of the new borders.*

ABOVE: *The herbaceous borders with the tulip tree beyond.*

LEFT: *The new herbaceous borders to the south of the swimming pool link. Their shape reflects the difficult modeling of the land.*

BELOW: *Sketch of croquet lawn and terrace.*

FOLLOWING PAGES: *The arbor encloses a very private space that will be hard to find once the climbers have grown up; the scented rose garden as viewed from the drawing room window.*

A LONDON GARDEN

This was an intriguing project that required an integration of the skills and imagination of the interior designer Joanna Wood, the architects Barrett Lloyd Davis, and myself. We had worked together before, but this was quite a formidable test of our ingenuity. There was not the scope for an extensive garden, but what we designed would have a particular impact on the interior, especially at basement level. We were fortunate in that the clients were young, and adventurous and between us we created an external space that comes as a wonderful surprise. It had been unpromisingly dark and unattractive; a pit that was surrounded on three sides by two-story buildings and on the west side by five stories. Now it is full of light and color, and gives the illusion of being far larger than its actual 27 square meters.

The size and shape of the space imposed great limitations on us, but also presented a terrific design challenge. One side was permanently in shade, and even where the sunlight did penetrate, it didn't stay for long. But the courtyard was of critical importance to the interior design of the lower floors, and we wanted to make the most of it. We gave the impression of a more generous space than was actually available by dividing the courtyard into three sections. This meant that the aspect from the conservatory that is attached to the kitchen was through trellis arches down to the covered seat on the garage wall. We used the finest natural materials outside, including sawn stone and planed and painted timbers, to complement the interior design. The garden furniture, seats, pots and lead water trough were all designed with the greatest care. And, of course, we also took pains to provide a rich growing medium in the beds so that the shrubs and climbers quickly and vigorously established themselves to extravagantly lush effect, especially on the trellis work. Despite the network of drains and services underground at this level, we were still able to create reasonably deep beds to support large shrubs such as *Acer palmatum*, *Skimmia foremanii*, *Pittosporum tenuifolium* and *viburnum x bodnantense*. And wreathing the trellis is white wisteria, trachelospemum, roses and clematis. As a final touch, we added dozens of handsome clay pots from the Landscape Ornament Company, which were filled with bays, box, marguerites, camellias and annuals.

We were unable to take full advantage of the possibilities presented by the terrace on the upper level because the required permissions to develop the roof space as a garden were unfortunately not available. Nonetheless it was a decent open area, which did not need to be blended with the interior, so we timber decked it, built fixed benches and put in planters and trellis work that now support shrubs such as *Fremontodendron californicum* and *Cytisus battandieri*, *Spartium junceum*, *Caryopteris x Clandonensis* and Rosemary, Lavender and Sage, and climbers include clematis, solanum, roses, honeysuckle, and hops.

ABOVE: *The use of trellis arches to create a succession of distinct areas giving the impression of more space. High quality furnishings are of the greatest importance in such a small area.*
RIGHT: *Garden plan.*

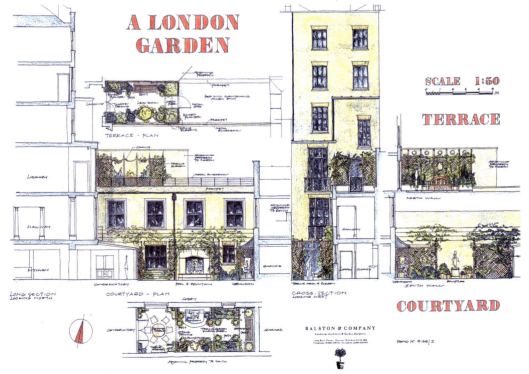

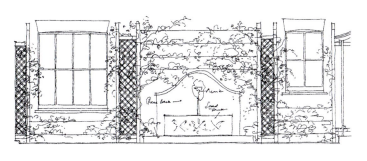

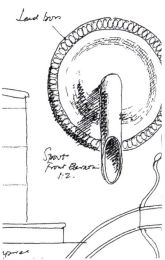

ABOVE: *Despite its unpromising situation, rich planting was achieved.*
TOP LEFT: *The lead tank and spout were custom made for the garden.*
LEFT: *Sketch for water feature and trellis.*
BELOW: *Sketch for water feature spout.*

THE GRANGE

One good garden design relationship can often give birth to another. My long involvement with Rofford Manor brought forth just such a commission. Following a visit to Rofford in 1994, Bill and Linda Caldwell were sufficiently inspired to entrust me with a fundamental redesign of their garden at The Grange, a village house in West Sussex.

The Grange occupies a pleasant southerly slope stretching from the village street to the River Rother and is about 1.15 hectares (2.84 acres) in size. The house is constructed in stone, rendered on the garden side, with brick dressings and a tiled roof. It is largely Georgian and has an engaging asymmetry. It has stone boundary walls, and its lawns running down to the river are dotted about with interesting trees and shrubs dating from the time of the previous owner, a keen plant collector. There is a wonderful low-lying valley landscape across the river. My brief was to capitalize on the existing garden, but to create more places—areas to sit, to enjoy different times of the day, different activities, views and plant combinations. My clients wanted to enjoy some of the variety that they had seen at Rofford.

The possibilities were endless but as in most designs it was necessary to exercise a partial process of elimination based on financial constraints. Other important considerations were future labor requirements and costs involved in the garden's upkeep. There is no point in creating an elaborate garden, however beautiful, if it cannot be maintained. The general thrust of the design was suggested by the assets already on site—the character of the house, the views, existing free-standing walls and retaining walls, and the excellent plants already in place. These factors tended to determine spaces, functions, and routes and my role was mostly one of reorganization bringing the whole garden into play, creating new kinds of spaces, and reinforcing the existing planting. As usual, I carried out a thorough survey and analysis of what was there. I then worked on different areas in a fairly loose sort of way to find how to make the most of them and at the same time best fit a coherent scheme.

In some designs there are overriding reasons for wholesale change, but this was not really one of them and a process of adjustments achieved better results. We worked up an overall plan fairly rapidly, followed by construction and planting details for each area as and when required. New planting areas were contained in a flow of shrubs and herbaceous perennials flowering throughout the year. But there were different emphases at different points—such as old-fashioned roses, mostly pink, near the entrance or the raised thyme lawn, rich purple in flower, on the lower terrace to the east. Off the conservatory terrace we created an oval lawn within the curve of an existing stone retaining wall, broken by a flight of steps leading down to a new croquet lawn. We planted these areas predominantly with shrubs but finished the design against the open lawns with a massive herbaceous border.

With clients keen on their horticulture and partially acid soil there is a greater range of plants here than in most other gardens I have undertaken. The flowering season is greatly improved and there are more durable textures. Spatially it seems a new garden and yet it holds on to all the principal elements that existed before. Over four years The Grange has achieved a new excitement of plant and place.

RIGHT: *Seats are so important in design—not only for a rest in the sun—but also as a focus of a layout.*
BELOW: *Preliminary study east of house.*
OPPOSITE PAGE: *Garden plan.*

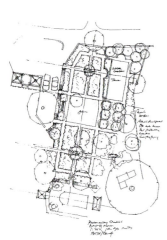

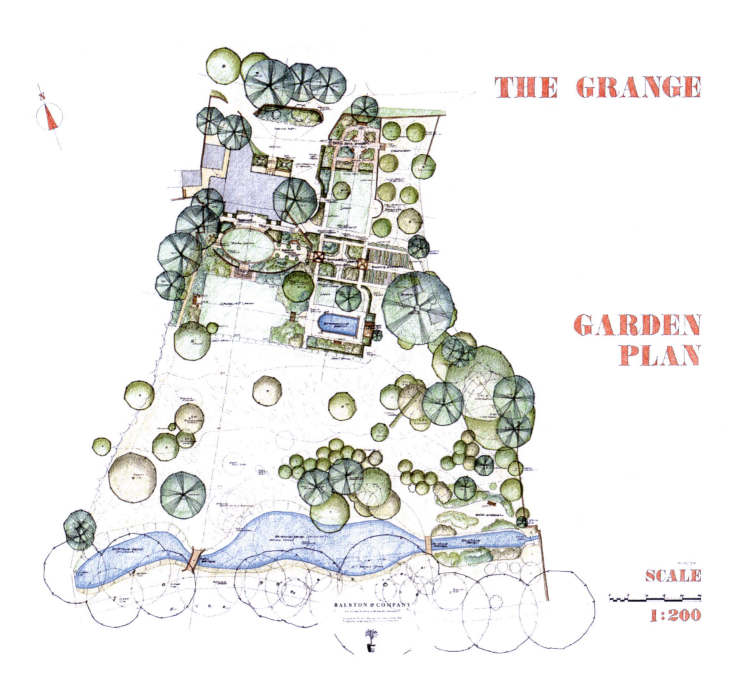

THE GRANGE

GARDEN
PLAN

SCALE

1:200

LEFT: *Urns are a useful contrast to plantings. Here in the planting bed, it defines an edge.*

OPPOSITE PAGE: *The long step flanks an oval lawn and leads down from the conservatory terrace.*

ABOVE: *Light and shade lead eye and foot from space to space.*

RIGHT: *The swimming pool was inherited from a previous scheme and planted around with shrubs to give privacy.*

ABOVE: *Plants that seem almost stemless like* Verbena bonariensis *are frequently used to give a light froth over a border.*

LEFT: *A view across the garden showing some of the mature trees and shrubs already on site.*

LEFT: *Perhaps the most telling feature of a good garden design is the manipulation of textures—so much more rewarding than the ephemeral of flowers.*

OPPOSITE PAGE: *Boxwood balls are useful for creating edges. In this case, they help define a path.*

FOLLOWING PAGES: *The pink-flecked lollipops of Rosa Heritage grown as standards create a unifying element on the axes of the rose garden.*

DAILY TELEGRAPH GARDEN

I have always been interested in show gardens, ever since I first exhibited at Chelsea in 1979. There is an enormous challenge in producing a convincing garden under show conditions, with limited build-up times and under intense professional and public scrutiny. For a variety of reasons I had not exhibited at Chelsea since 1986. During the interval the show had changed pretty dramatically. In particular, with corporate sponsorship, budgets had were significantly bigger and Chelsea had become a media event. However, I really only wanted to exhibit at Chelsea if I could design something that was forward-looking, using modern materials and not overburdened by tradition. Also, I wanted to be sure that the garden would be re-used after the show. It took some time to find the right sponsor, but eventually the Editor Charles Moore asked me to create a modern garden for the 1999 Show on behalf of *The Daily Telegraph*.

I had long been interested in tensile structures and admired the work of Frei Otto and Buro Happold and the way so many good modern architects use them in buildings. I felt that, at a small scale, they had an obvious application in gardens. For a show garden such structures could be used more in a dynamic, sculptural way than in a purely functional way. I thus developed a plan in which light canopies created a tension and movement that was picked up both in the structural elements, such as steps and decking, and in the diagonal lay of the planting. Although it was a minute garden, it was one of the most exciting that I had ever worked on. And it greatly helped to have an enlightened sponsor backing me all the way, as well as having the able technical expertise of Buro Happold to make the structures stand up.

The diagonal movement overlay a longitudinal organization. On one side was a decking walkway to make people feel as though they were actually inside the garden as they passed under the canopies. Next was a canal in three descending sections with a stepped lawn alongside opening out to the front and focusing on the elliptical stainless steel sanctuary at the rear with its flared trumpet-like canopy. Next to the lawn was a mixed border in which strong textural clumps picked up the booms of the canopies opposite. The design was an exercise in dynamic counterpoint, contained within a powerful, but light, framework in which deliberate contrasts between line and mass, texture and color, were exploited to create layers of interpenetrating spaces.

While the design was developing, I was approached by the curator of the RHS garden at Wisley, Jim Gardiner, to submit a garden for the Wisley Show Gardens area, and arrange for its sponsorship. Quite unexpectedly, here was the second use I was looking for. Thanks to further funding from *The Daily Telegraph*, the garden is now installed on a new site and looking better than ever. The advantage of the Wisley site is that it is on a significant slope so that you approach the garden from below coming up under the canopies. The vertical dimension seems to be more powerful.

For Chelsea, apart from the textural anchors, I concentrated on plants that could be in flower in the penultimate week in May such as *Cercis siliquastrum, Cornus kousa* and a variety of Rhododendrons like Souvenir de President Carnot, Daviesii, and Persil. We included climbing roses and used good sub-shrubs like Epimediums and Euphorbias. The taller herbaceous plants, like Irises, foxgloves and day lilies, emphasized the diagonal lay, while geraniums, Primula and Heuchera and masses of hostas and ferns ran under the shrubs. It was a deliberately rich melange pinned down by strong textural clumps of phormium, yucca and rosemary. It set off the spare framework of steel blue masts and white canopies to perfection.

For Wisley we thinned out the planting considerably and added plants to perform well at other times of the year. Some of the rhododendrons for instance disappeared to allow space for the remaining plants to grow. The garden is now in the capable hands of David Jewel and his staff and the planting is racing away giving it a precocious maturity. I have agreed with David that he should move plants in or take plants out as required. I firmly believe that the garden should not only be able to cope with change, but should actually welcome it. Gardening is a temporal art as well as a spatial one. Gardeners should be encouraged to experiment with plants. My role as a designer is to provide an inspiring structure within which these plants are used.

TOP: *Computer model.*
ABOVE: *The garden installed at Wisley.*

DAILY TELEGRAPH GARDEN   CHELSEA 1999

ABOVE: *The precision of the masts and booms on the viewer's side of the garden contrasts strongly with the billowing masses of vegetation.*

TOP LEFT: *The steps in the grass create a sense of space and distance in the small space of the garden. Plantings are chosen that flower at the end of May during the Chelsea Flower Show.*

LEFT: *Garden plan.*

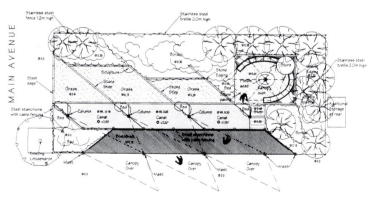

GARDEN WAY

Dwg no B222-10A
BALSTON & COMPANY
Long Barn, Patney, Devizes, Wiltshire SN10 3RB

SCALE 1:100

Date of Completion:
Ongoing
Photographers: Michael
Balston, James Balston

Little Malvern Court
Little Malvern,
Worcestershire, England

Client: Mrs. & Mrs. T.M.
Berington
Date of Completion: 1988
Contractor: M. Walsh &
Son (Malvern) Ltd.
Photographers: Michael
Balston, James Balston

Jannaways
Berkshire, England

Client: The Hon. & Mrs.
Christopher Sharples
Date of Completion: 1987
(ongoing)
Contractor: Thames Water
Photographers: Michael
Balston, James Balston

Client: Mr. & Mrs. J.
Mogford
Date of Completion: 1989
(ongoing)
Landscape Contractor:
Client organization
Photographers: Michael
Balston, James Balston

Cucklington House
Somerset, England

Client: Private
Date of Completion: 1994
General Contractor:
Bayford Builders, Ltd.
Groundworks Contractor:
Newbridge Plant Services
(1984) Ltd.
Landscape Contractor:
Johnstone Landscapes &
client staff
Photographers: Michael
Balston, James Balston

Heather's Farm
West Sussex, England

Client: Mr. & Mrs. C.

Murwest Services AG
Landscape Contractor:
Landmark
Photographers: Michael
Balston, James Balston

Lower Lye
Somerset, England

Client: Mr. & Mrs. A.
Scott
Date of Completion: 1996
Architects: Nicholas
Johnston & Peter Cave
Associates
General Contractor:
G. J. Smith Bros.
Groundworks Contractor:
Mike Lock Construction:
Landscape Contractor:
Bob Carter
Photographers: Michael
Balston, James Balston

A London Garden
London

Client: Private
Date of Completion: 1995

Photographers: Michael
Balston, James Balston

The Grange
West Sussex, England

Client: Mr. & Mrs. W.
Caldwell
Date of completion: 1997
Contractor: Client staff
Photographers: Michael
Balston, James Balston

Daily Telegraph Garden
Wisley, Surrey

Client: The Daily
Telegraph
Date of Completion: 1999
Landscape Contractor:
Hillier Landscapes
Consulting Engineers:
Buro Happold
Engineering Contractor:
Landrell Fabric
Engineering
Photographers: Jerry
Harpur, Michael Balston,
James Balston

FIRM PROFILE

Michael Balston studied architecture at Cambridge University, qualifying as an architect in the early 1970s. He then further qualified as a landscape architect and worked for Robert Mathew Johnson-Marshall & Partners on several public building projects in the United Kingdom and Saudi Arabia. In 1978, he joined Arabella Lennox Boyd to focus on private gardens and increase his knowledge of horticulture. Since moving to Wiltshire in 1983, Michael Balston has run his own practice operating from converted farm buildings within a large garden that he has created from scratch.

Over nearly 20 years, the company has developed significant experience on most aspects of landscape design and management. The core garden projects continue, ranging from rooftops to large estates. There is also a substantial portfolio of prominent urban design projects including housing rehabilitation, office landscapes, and public open spaces. Garden furniture production also continues to be an important activity. The emphasis on good horticulture combined with wide ranging architectural experience helps to produce imaginative and stimulating design. The company makes extensive use of computer techniques to explore design possibilities and provide fully illustrated and specified solutions.

Winning the Royal Horticultural Society's 'Best Garden' award at the 1999 Chelsea Flower show for his design for 'The Daily Telegraph Reflective Garden' was an important milestone in Michael Balston's attempts to make use of sophisticated engineering techniques and materials in gardens. For two decades he has won medals at national and international shows and this year he was responsible for the highly successful British exhibit at the quinquennial Floralies at Ghent. The gardens created at his own home in Wiltshire are his working laboratory. They have been widely featured in the gardening press. Besides writing for magazines, Michael Balston has written the influential book *The Well Furnished Garden*. He is much involved with The Royal Horticultural Society shows as a judge and member of the Chelsea Garden Panel. Returning to his architectural roots, he is also currently the UK judge on the Europa Nostra Awards panel.